Why is a zoo ca[...] Zoo is short for zoological (zoh-oh-LA-ji-kal), which means "having to do with animals."

Giraffes at Lincoln Park Zoo in Chicago, Illinois

A zoo is a place where people can see all kinds of living animals.

Animals in the Zoo

By Allan Fowler

Consultants
Linda Cornwell, Coordinator of School Quality
and Professional Improvement
Indiana State Teachers Association

Janann V. Jenner, Ph.D.

Children's Press®
A Division of Grolier Publishing
New York   London   Hong Kong   Sydney
Danbury, Connecticut

Designer: Herman Adler Design Group
Photo Researcher: Caroline Anderson

The photo on the cover shows a girl holding hands with
a koala bear at Taronga Zoo in Sydney, Australia.

Library of Congress Cataloging-in-Publication Data

Fowler, Allan.
  Animals in the zoo / by Allan Fowler.
     p. cm. — (Rookie read-about science)
  Includes index.
  Summary: Examines a variety of zoo animals and their housing,
including parrots, bears, gorillas, and killer whales.
     ISBN 0-516-21218-4 (lib. bdg.)   0-516-27087-7 (pbk.)
     1. Zoo animals—Juvenile literature. [1. Zoo animals. 2. Zoos.]
  I. Title. II. Series.
QL77.5.F68   2000
636.088'9—dc21   98-52942
                                                      CIP
                                                       AC

A hamadras baboon at the Bronx Zoo in New York, New York

An elephant at the Lincoln Park Zoo in Chicago, Illinois

Some of the animals are big.

Some are small.

Wild pigeons steal food given to prairie dogs.

Some are fierce.

Female lions at the Houston Zoo in Houston, Texas

A mother Mongolian wild horse with her colt

Some are friendly.

Two red pandas at the Bronx Zoo in New York, New York

Some are shy.

Some are show-offs.

A young gorilla

Some you will know.

A young grizzly bear takes a bath.

A capybara at the Bronx Zoo in New York, New York

Some will be new.

In some zoos, different kinds of animals are kept in different places.

All the birds are in one area. Apes and monkeys are in a different area.

A parrot at Parrot Jungle in Florida

These African animals live at a zoo in the United States.

In other zoos, animals live in places that are like their natural homes.

Mammals, birds, and reptiles live together— just as they do in the natural world.

A tropical rain forest building might have trees, ferns, a stream, and all kinds of rain forest animals.

As you walk through the building, you feel as if you are in a real rain forest.

This is a zoo, not a tropical rain forest.

A girl pets a goat at a zoo.

Some zoos have a special area with animals that you can pet.

Sea animals are kept in
a kind of zoo called a
marine park.

At some marine parks,
dolphins, killer whales,
and seals perform
in shows.

A killer whale performs tricks for people at a marine park.

Many baby animals are born in zoos. They are raised with great care.

A young polar bear

A zoo worker feeds a young hippo.

Zoo animals are given only healthy foods, and in just the right amounts.

That's why you should always obey the signs that read, "Don't feed the animals."

A monkey at a zoo

Words You Know

fierce

friendly

marine park

show-off

shy

tropical rain forest

zoo

Index

About the Author

Allan Fowler is a freelance writer with a background in advertising. Born in New York, he now lives in Chicago and enjoys traveling.

Photo Credits